Les numéros hors-série Beaux-Arts magazine sont édités par Beaux Arts SA.

Président-Directeur général :
Charles-Henri Flammarion.
Directeur de la publication :
Jean-Christophe Delpierre.
Directeur de la rédaction : Fabrice Bousteau.
Rédacteur en chef adjoint :
Mickaël Faure, assisté de Laurence Castany.
Secrétaire général de la rédaction :
Hortense Meltz.
Conception graphique :
Claire Luxey, sur une idée de Rudi Baur.
Iconographe : Agnès Cuchet.
Secrétaires de rédaction :
Isabelle Arson et, pour les versions étrangères,
Isabelle Gilloots.
Les commentaires d'œuvres
ont été rédigés par Nicole Barbier
et Antoinette Le Normand-Romain.
Traduction anglaise : Lisa Davidson.
Traduction italienne : Claire Lesage.
**Traductions japonaise, russe, espagnole
et allemande :** société SVP.
Directeur de la création et de la fabrication :
Alain Alliez, assisté de
Marie-France Wolfsperger.
Marketing : Isabelle Canals-Noël.
Tél. : 01 56 54 12 35.
Diffusion : Manon Courbez.
Tél. : 01 56 54 12 32.

**Beaux Arts magazine, tour Montparnasse,
33, av. du Maine, 75755 Paris, Cedex 15.**
Tél. : 01 56 54 12 34. Fax : 01 45 38 30 01.
RCS Paris B 404 332 942. ISSN : 0757 - 2271.
Dépôt légal : juin 2001.
Impression : Mariogros, Turin.

Nous remercions Stéphanie Le Follic
et Jean-Luc Pichon du musée Rodin
pour l'aide qu'ils ont apportée à la réalisation
de cet ouvrage.

1

Preface

by Jacques Vilain, director of the Rodin museum

CONTENTS

All photographs by
Bruno Jarret Adam Rzepka
are credited © ADAGP.
All the works represented
are credited © Musée Rodin,
unless otherwise specified.

Cover: **The Danaïde,**
1889-92, marble,
36 x 71 x 53 cm. Inv. S. 1155.
© Photo D. Boudinet.

Pages 2-3 and 66-67:
**Rodin installing the
plaster of
Contorted Hand** with
Imploring Figure,
anonymous photograph,
16.7 x 11.7 cm.

1 **The Thinker** (1880-1882)
from The Gates of Hell
(cast between 1919 and
1929), bronze. S 1304.
© Photo D. Boudinet.

The works of Auguste Rodin have become universal symbols. There is no need to mention Beethoven when discussing *The Pastorale*, Balzac in reference to *La Comédie humaine*, or Berlioz when listening to *La Symphonie fantastique*. The same is true for Rodin: *The Gates of Hell, The Monument to Balzac, The Burghers of Calais, The Thinker* and *The Kiss* are all such masterpieces that they have little need of their creator's name to be immediately identifiable. However, Rodin had to wait many years before he was recognized by both the art establishment and the general public. It was not until the 1880s, after the scandal stirred up by the Age of Bronze exhibition, that he was recognized as a truly great artist. The culmination of his career was probably in 1900 when he exhibited the best of his work at the Pavillon de l'Alma. He was then sixty years old. Although Rodin liked to live in Meudon in modest surroundings, early on he dreamed of creating a museum in the luxurious Hôtel Biron, a unique setting right in the middle of Paris, surrounded by seven acres of garden. This museum was to be dedicated to his work as well as to his personal collections. After some hard-fought battles, the Rodin Museum opened its doors in 1919, two years after the sculptor's death.

Thus, the belated but resounding recognition of his work occurred within this setting; ever since, the museum has welcomed admirers of these masterpieces of universal sculpture.

The Rodin Museum

At number 77 rue de Varenne stands the Hôtel Biron, not one of the traditional faubourg Saint-Germain homes with a courtyard and garden, but a real château standing in the middle of its own grounds. Indeed, this was how it was envisaged by Abraham Peyrenc de Moras, the man who commissioned it. A wigmaker who became wealthy speculating in paper money, Moras commissioned architect Jean Aubert – who later built the luxurious château de Chantilly – to draw up the plans. The speed of its construction (1729-30) no doubt explains the architectural unity of the building, one of the most beautiful examples of the Rococo style. The refinement of detail on the facade is set off by the clear lines of the south-facing salons inside, as well as by the magnificent light that cuts across the building from the entrance and the three French windows facing the terrace overlooking the grounds. A demanding customer, Peyrenc de Moras commissioned a series of wood panels of rare quality. From the painter François Lemoine, who was later to paint the ceiling of the Hercule Salon at Versailles, he ordered a series of magnificent Rococo cornices and door panels. Two of these have been recently acquired and returned to their original setting.

Peyrenc de Moras hardly had time to enjoy his luxurious home as he died in 1732. His widow then rented it to the duchesse du Maine, Louis XIV's daughter-in-law, until her death in 1753. The property was then sold to the maréchal de Biron, hero of the battle of Fontenoy, and was to carry his name from that moment on. Biron did little to change the original appearance of the hôtel, concentrating instead on the grounds: he added statues, grottos, pavilions, ponds and a patchwork of borders containing the rarest of plants. The grounds – some of the most beautifully maintained of the period – were greatly admired by visitors to the hôtel. On Biron's death

2 **North side
of the Hôtel Biron.**
Photo J. Manoukian.

3 **Rodin wearing
a felt hat,**
photograph by
Pierre Choumoff,
23 x 17.1 cm. Inv. Ph 34.

in 1788, the estate was left to his nephew, the duc de Lauzun. Although the duc participated in the American War of Independence and commanded the revolutionary army of the Rhine, he was guillotined in 1793.

The Revolution also brought about a decline in the estate's fortunes. The grounds were rented out for public festivities and dances. The splendid flower beds disappeared and were replaced by a fairground. Under the Consulate and later the Empire, the Hôtel Biron once again became a palatial residence, housing first the papal delegation, then the Russian embassy. After her death, the pious duchesse de Béthune-Chârost, who owned the estate, wanted the hôtel to fulfill a purpose in keeping with her own religious principles. In 1820 she therefore donated it to the Société du Sacré-Cœur de Jésus (founded in 1804), dedicated to the proper education of young girls of the aristocracy. Run by its founder, Mother Sophie Barat, the boarding-school had a reputation for quality education,

strict rules and well-bred students. Eugénie de Montijo studied there before marrying Napoléon III. Mother Barat conducted a purge against all things frivolous and luxurious; the disastrous consequence of this policy meant the sale by the congregation of all superfluous ornaments, wainscoting, mirrors, ironwork and painted cornices.

In 1905, with the separation of Church and State, the estate fell into civil hands, but it was in a dire condition. Robbed of its wonderful decoration, surrounded by an overrun gardens, the hôtel was in a sad state. The future of the hôtel and its grounds became uncertain; logically, the hôtel should have been demolished and the gardens developed. However, the agent responsible for liquidating the property agreed to allow a few tenants to temporary move into the building and its outbuildings. Fortunately, this temporary situation continued and the hôtel Biron was saved. Illustrious occupants of the hôtel included

4 **Rodin sculpting next to a female model,** photograph attributed to Duchene, 24.5 x 16.3 cm. Inv. Ph. 2005.

5 *Crouching Woman,* 1882, terracotta, 25.5 x 21 x 21 cm. Inv. S. 109. Photo E. and P. Hesmerg.

6 **Rodin sitting in a room of the Hôtel Biron,** photography by Lémery, 18 x 24.5 cm. Inv. Ph. 196.

6

Jean Cocteau, Matisse and, of course, Rodin, who moved into the south rooms on the ground floor in 1908 on the advice of poet Rainer Maria Rilke. Although he continued to live and work at Meudon, Rodin liked to spend time in Paris and organized soirées in this historic building.

The fate of the hôtel Biron was not, however, definitively settled. The risk of demolition was still a real one. In 1911, the State took possession of the property and divided it; the southern section was split off and given to the Victor Duruy lycée. At this point arose the idea of transforming the building into the Rodin Museum. The project generated a great deal of opposition, as the sculptor's art at this period was misunderstood and even considered provocative. Monet, Mirabeau, Poincaré, Clémenceau, Clémentel and others intervened on his behalf, and the project was finally approved on December 22, 1916.

Rodin donated his collections, archives, all of his works, sculptures and drawings, along with the rights to them to the State. The museum opened its doors in l919. Rodin died on November 17, 1917, and never saw the realization of what was to be his final project. **Jacques Vilain**

9

8

7 *Dawn,*
ca. 1882-84, plaster,
24.6 x 17.2 x 27 cm.
Inv. S. 1994.
Photo E. and P. Hesmerg.
© Musée Rodin / SPADEM.

8 **The Hôtel Biron**
viewed from the garden,
anonymous photograph,
17 x 22.6 cm. Inv. Ph. 1367.

9 **Camille Claudel,**
Les Causeuses,
1897, onyx and bronze,
44.9 x 42.2 x 39 cm.
Inv. S. 1006.
Photo E. and P. Hesmerg.
© Musée Rodin / SPADEM.

The Sculpture Garden

11

The garden of the Hôtel Biron occupies just over seven acres; it includes a rose garden to the north of the house and a large flowerbed to the south, which was re-landscaped in 1993. Several projects were considered at the time: to restore the box hedging that decorated the garden in the eighteenth century, or to recreate the untamed space of Rodin's time, when the garden was overrun with brambles and wild apple trees, under which rabbits scurried, "like in a medieval tapestry," as Rilke once wrote. Jacques Sgard's proposal was finally selected: while retaining the basin, the expanse of lawn and the rows of lime trees, he recreated the naturalist theme that was so popular in the eighteenth century.

Many sculptures have been placed throughout this new space. *Adam*, *Eve*, *Meditation* and *The Spirit of Eternal Rest* surround the basin and a number of bronzes have been added: *Orpheus*, *Whistler's Muse*, *Bastien Lepage*, *The Three Shadows*, *The Two Caryatids* and the large studies for *The Burghers of Calais* gradually took over the remaining space. Exhibitions of contemporary sculpture were organized in the garden, including "Homage to the Lime Trees and to Rodin," by François Morellet.

The first bronzes were placed in the gardens before the First World War. *The Thinker*, offered by a group of admirers in 1906 to be placed in front of the Pantheon, was transferred with its base to the Rodin Museum in 1922. In 1927, an enlargement of *Ugolin* was installed in the middle of the basin, followed by a second copy of *The Gates of Hell*, cast in 1929, but only set up in 1937, along with *The Burghers* of Calais the same year. *Balzac*, which is an old casting

10 **The large basin in the garden.**
Photo B. Jarret.

11 **Facade of the Hôtel Biron facing the garden.**
Photo I. Bissière.

12 **The Thinker,**
1880-1904,
bronze, 180 x 98 x 145 cm.
Inv. S. 1295. Photo B. Jarret.

(made before 1936), was placed in the garden much later. There are also several marbles in the sculpture garden. The most important of these include *Monument to Victor Hugo*, inaugurated in 1909 in the gardens of the Palais-Royal, and removed in 1933 when it was transferred to the Rodin Museum. Subject to the effects of humidity, the marbles became covered with moss and began to show signs of wear. A decision was taken in 1995 to placed them under shelter in the Marble Gallery, now enclosed with large bay windows. Visitors today can admire the sculptures from the outside, while the leaves and facade of the building reflected in the windows create a poetic ambiance.

This new presentation meant that more works could be exhibited and that sculptures could be grouped together by theme. The last section is therefore devoted to *Victor Hugo*, the figure of the poet surrounded by *The Tragic Muse*, who leans over to breath inspiration into his ear. This is how the original project for the monument was exhibited in 1897. The bronze sculptures are carefully maintained to preserve the old patina. These efforts, which began in 1993 with the sculpture of Balzac, have been expanded to include all of the sculptures in the garden.
Antoinette Le Normand-Romain

13 **The Three Shades,**
ca. 1882-1902, bronze,
191.5 x 191.8 x 115 cm.
Inv. S.6411. Photo A. Rzepka.

14 **Inside of the Marble Gallery in the gardens of the museum.**
Photo E. and P. Hesmerg.

13

14

Preceding double page:
The Gates of Hell, detail.
1880-1917, bronze, 635 x 400 x 85 cm.
Inv. S. 1304. Photo B. Jarret.

16 **The Age of Bronze,**
1877, bronze, 181 x 66.5 x 63 cm.
Inv. S. 986. Photo E. and P. Hesmerg.

This work was highly criticized
when it was first exhibited
in 1977 in Belgium, where it was
created. Rodin was accused
of making a cast from a live
model. Convinced that the sculptor
had not done so, Turquet,
undersecretary of state for the
Beaux-Arts, commissioned a
bronze cast of *The Age of Bronze*
for the Musée de Luxembourg.
The transition into bronze
accentuated the extraordinary
precision of the sculpting, which is
equaled only by the Florentine
Renaissance masters.
Rodin, who had just returned from
a trip to Italy, expressed enormous
admiration for their work.

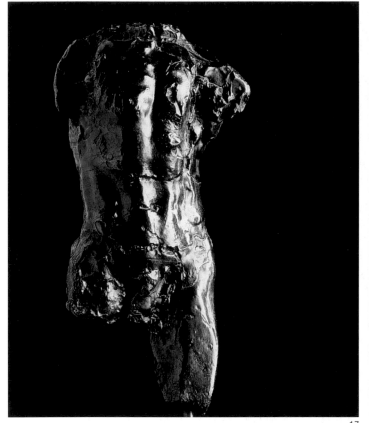

17 **Study for *The Walking Man,***
ca. 1870, bronze, 53 x 27 x 15 cm.
Inv. S. 602. Photo E. and P. Hesmerg.

18 ***The Walking Man,***
1900-07, bronze,
213.5 x 71.7 x 156.5 cm.
Inv. S. 998. Photo B. Jarret.

Rodin probably composed
this deeply innovative work
– which broke with the sculpture of
his own time – using separate
segments created when
he was working on *Saint John the
Baptist:* studies of legs from
the model and torsos from antique
busts. Rodin revealed the
expressive capacity of the body,
stripped to its essential
volumes. At the same time, he
broke with the classical
tradition that only accepted
a perfect and whole representation
of the human body.
The Walking Man, with its
foot firmly planted on the ground,
suggests the sequence and
permanence of movements
and progress through space, all
extremely modern ideas
that would be developed
in the 20th century. Exhibited
for the first time in 1900,
this work received a definitive title
only in 1907, when it
was enlarged to two meters and
cast in bronze.

19

19 and 20 **The Thinker,**
1880-1904, bronze, 180 x 98 x 145 cm.
Inv. S. 1292. Photo J. Manoukian.

This is one of Rodin's most
well-known sculptures.
A smaller version was first made
in 1880 for *The Gates of Hell*,
where it reigned in the
middle of the tympanum.
It represents Dante reflecting on
his poetic creation and symbolizes
the "creator" in general.
Rodin planned to enlarge
it in 1902. After exhibiting the work
in the 1904 Salon, a public
subscription was opened
so that a bronze could be installed
in a public place in Paris.
Set up in 1906 in front of
the Pantheon, it was considered
to be too small for its
surroundings and was returned
to the Rodin Museum
in 1922. It now stands in the
garden, in the midst
of a grove of pruned yew trees.

21 *The Kiss,*
1882-98, marble,
183.6 x 110.5 x 118.3 cm. Inv. S. 1002.
Photo E. and P. Hesmerg.

This embracing couple represents
Paolo and Francesca, figures
from Dante's masterpiece. It is one
of the groups created for
The Gates of Hell. Rodin removed
it from this project in 1886.
This first version was exhibited in
1887 and called *The Kiss*
by critics. It was so successful that
the government commissioned the
marble for the 1889
Universal Exhibition. Yet it was not
exhibited before 1898, at the
same time as *Balzac*, and again in
1900. It was extremely
popular: two marble copies were
made and are now in London and
Copenhagen, along with many
smaller bronze copies
by Barbedienne. Rodin felt that
the work was still highly
academic; yet today, *The Kiss*
symbolizes Rodin's sculpture.

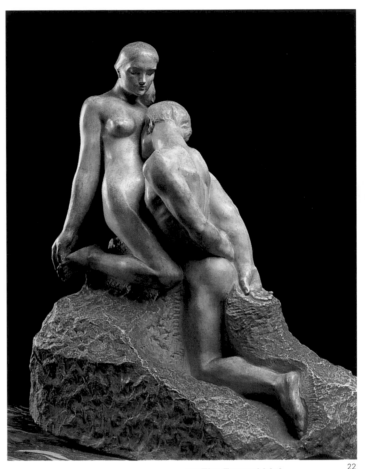

22

22 *The Eternal Idol,*
ca. 1889, plaster, 73.2 x 59.2 x 41.1 cm.
Inv .S. 1044. Photo B. Jarret.

The title of this work underlines
the importance of the "female
inspiration" for Rodin, also
celebrated by the Symbolist
writers. The sculpture was
probably made in the late 1880s,
while Rodin was working
repeatedly on the theme of the
kiss. The two figures reappear
together or separately in
several compositions: they can be
seen embracing in the
hollow of the arms of one of the
Damned on *The Gates
of Hell*, visible in the lovely
terra-cotta study entitled *Creation.*

23 *Je suis belle*,
1886, bronze, 69 x 36 x 36 cm.
Inv. S. 1151. Photo B. Jarret.

This group, formed of two figures
from *The Gates of Hell*
– *The Falling Man* and *The
Crouching Woman* – and exhibited
after 1886 as a "study of human
rutting," is one of the finest
examples of "assemblage" in
Rodin's work. It was originally titled
"*Enlèvement*," as if to accentuate
the savagery that seems
to overwhelm the two figures,
but its definitive title
came from a poem by Baudelaire
(for whom Rodin illustrated
Les Fleurs du mal): "Je suis belle,
ô mortels, comme un rêve
de pierre…"

24 Camille Claudel,
The Walz,
1893-95, bronze, 43.2 x 23 x 34.3 cm.
Inv. S 1013. Photo B. Jarret.
© Musée Rodin / SPADEM.

The figures in the group, initially
nude as in Rodin's *Kiss*, were
considered shocking because of
"the violent reality that …
prevents it … from being placed in
a gallery open to the public."
Camille Claudel then added
the drapery, which accentuated the
bold and skillful imbalance
of the composition. Highly praised
when it was exhibited in 1893,
The Waltz was the first in
a series of ambitious and intimate
works created by the artist.

25 Camille Claudel,
Vertumne and Pomone,
1888-1905, marble, 92 x 80 x 42.5 cm.
Inv. S. 1293. Photo E. and P. Hesmerg.
© Musée Rodin / SPADEM.

This marble, donated by Paul Claudel
to the Rodin Museum in 1952, was
first called *Sakountala* (after a
Hindu legend), then *Abandon*. It is
perfectly balanced and reflects the
artist's infinitely subtle sculpting
technique. It has often been
compared to Rodin's works
(*The Kiss* and *The Eternal Idol*) but
the importance attributed to
the spirit makes it quite different.

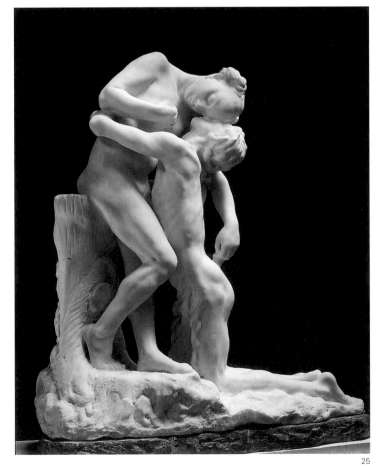

26 and 27 **The Burghers of Calais,**
1884-89, bronze, 231 x 245 x 203 cm,
and details of the hands.
Inv. S. 450. Photo J. Manoukian.

In 1884, the city of Calais
commissioned a monument from
Rodin in honor of the
six burghers who were to sacrifice
their lives to save their village
besieged by the English during the
Hundred Years' War. The sculptor
chose the most dramatic moment,
when the burghers were walking
toward the king in the enemy
camp, as each one reflected on his
own death. Exhibited in the garden
of the museum, the sculpture of
The Burghers of Calais was set at
ground level, according to Rodin's
wishes. The city of Calais, where
the monument was inaugurated in
1895, preferred a traditional
presentation with the group on a
high pedestal. Rodin wanted it to be
at eye level to reduce the distance
between the sculpted figures
and people viewing the work, and
to emphasize the dramatic
appearance of the group.
Each burgher has a characteristic
gesture, with his hand either open
or closed. Rodin freely altered
the proportions of the hands and
legs, overdeveloping them to
reinforce the dramatic impact, an
effect he also attained by
creating the strong areas of shadow.
Young man or old, each figure
becomes an archetype of a sacrifice
devoted to a common cause.

28 **Pierre de Wissant nude in the studio,**
photograph by Charles Bodmer,
ca. 1886, 25.3 x 21.5 cm. Inv. Ph. 322.

29 *The Burghers of Calais,*
1885, plaster, 71.5 x 78 x 70.2 cm.
Inv. S. 88/89/90/91/413/434.
Photo B. Hatala.

Rodin worked on this monument in several stages. In the first maquette, he stressed the collective expression of sacrifice. He then made nude and clothed studies for each figure, which resulted in a second maquette in 1885, made to one-third the final dimensions. Each figure in the group is unique either through his age, attitude or expression. The municipal authorities of Calais, however, did not appreciate the composition or the feeling of discouragement it expressed. Despite this criticism and bankruptcy of the bank holding the subscription bonds, Rodin continued his research. He studied the nudes, heads and hands separately before finally creating the definitive figures. The full-size plaster model was exhibited in 1895.

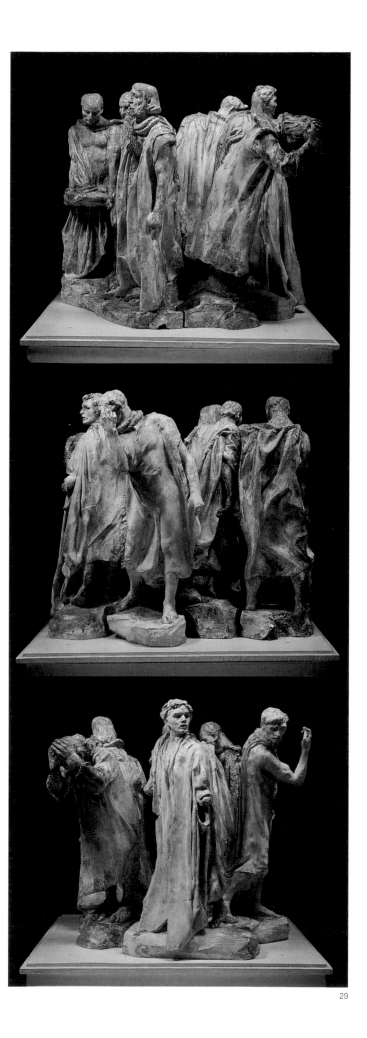

31 **The Danaïde,**
1889-92, marble, 36 x 71 x 53 cm.
Inv. S. 1155. © Photo D.Boudinet.

Rodin had the idea for this *Danaïde*
– a desperate young woman
condemned to pour water forever
into a bottomless vase – while
working on the themes of *The
Gates of Hell*. It is one of the most
beautiful marbles (sculpted by
Escoula) created in Rodin's studio.
The fully exposed and admirably
sculpted back extends
from the "liquid" hair (Rilke).
The many copies of this work
attest to its success.

30

30 **Paolo and Francesca,**
ca. 1905, marble, 81 x 108 x 65 cm.
Inv. S. 1423. Photo B. Jarret.

The theme of the damned lovers,
so often sculpted by Rodin,
is here again a pretext for
presenting two embracing figures.
This marble is also typical of
Rodin's research during this period,
which systematized the
opposition between the smooth
and rough sections, and multiplied
the various ways of treating
the surface, some parts of which
even look unfinished.
The figures occupy only a small
section of the composition in
comparison with the abstract block
of marble that catches the light.

34 *le Sommeil*,
1889-94, marble,
48.4 x 56 x 47.5 cm. Inv. S. 1004.
Photo B. Jarret.

This undated bust, in which
an opposition is created between
the barely roughed-out stone
and the sensitive sculpting of the
face, was made from a remarkable,
half-colored, plaster and
terra-cotta maquette. It consisted
of an assemblage of a bust,
a right hand and part of a wreath,
which became indistinct
when the marble was sculpted.

32 *The Prodigal Son*,
1884-94, bronze,
138.2 x 99.8 x 69 cm.
Inv. S. 1130. Photo A. Rzepka.

"I accentuated the muscles
to express distress.
Here and there I exaggerated
the separation of
the tendons that mark the energy
of the prayer..." This is
how Rodin explained
the transformation of a male figure
from *The Gates of Hell*
(in the *Fugit Amor* group) into
The Prodigal Son,
one of his works
which most strongly expresses
unbridled despair.

33

33 *Illusion, Icarus' Sister*,
1896, marble, 62 x 96 x 51 cm.
Inv. S. 1385. Photo B. Jarret.

One of the figures most often
sculpted by Rodin,
The Martyr can be recognized
in this work, this time
winged and overturned.
This marble was exhibited in the
1896 Salon and was therefore
contemporaneous with
the break between Camille Claudel
and Rodin; indeed, the bitter
title is certainly an echo
of this event, while the figure
was inspired from
Ovid's *Metamorphosis* (*Alcyon
Transformed into a Bird*).

32

35 The Centauress,
1901-04, marble,
70.4 x 103.9 x 32 cm. Inv. S 1031.
Photo B. Hatala.

Rodin drew and modeled centaurs
incessantly while he was working
on *The Gates of Hell*.
The original plaster of this work,
made sometime around 1887,
already has traces of the
assemblage technique that the
sculptor would later use
systematically to compose figures.
Rodin used the body of
the horse from *Monument to
General Lynch*, to which
he added a female torso, the head
of the woman from *Fugit
Amor*, and arms stretched upward.

36 Iris, Messenger of the Gods,
ca. 1890-91,
bronze, 82.1 x 86.3 x 52 cm.
Inv. S. 1068. Photo B. Jarret.

This work is one of the most
audacious in a series
that also includes *Flying Figure* and
Seated Female Torso.
Rodin was able to balance the
sculpture by extending
the arms and legs into space; he
did not have to use a base
incorporated into the bronze. This
version is even more powerful than
the work with a head, as here,
all the strength is in the movement
of the wide-open legs.

36

37 **Monument to Balzac,**
1891-98, bronze,
270 x 120.5 x 128 cm. Inv. S. 1296.
© Photo D. Boudinet.

38 **The Open Sky, 11 p. m. (Balzac),**
photo Edward Steichen,
49 x 36 cm. Inv. Ph. 233.

In 1883 the Société des gens de
lettres opened a subscription
to create a monument to Balzac;
the commission for the work
was given to the sculptor Chapu.
After his death in 1891, Rodin was
asked to create the work.
The sculptor made numerous
studies before deciding to
represent the writer clad in his
dressing gown. The work
was exhibited at the Salon de la
Société nationale des Beaux-Arts in
1898, where was received
with hostility from the model,
while the committee of the Société
des gens de lettres refused
the work. The bold simplification
and the expressive strength of
Rodin's *Balzac* made it a forerunner
of 20th-century sculpture.

38

39 and 40 **The Hand of God,**
1896-1916, marble, 95.5 x 75 x 56 cm.
Inv. S. 988. Photo E. and P. Hesmerg.

The expressive power in this work
makes this one of Rodin's
most famous sculptures. For
Rodin, the hand that sculpts was
indeed an instrument of creation
par excellence. According to Rodin,
"The first thing God thought
of when He created the world, if
we can imagine God's thoughts, is
the form; it's funny, don't you
think, to make of God a sculptor?"
And as if to echo this idea,
a small female torso, sculpted by
Rodin, was placed in the cast
of a hand that had been made by
Paul Cruet, several weeks before
his death. The first version
of *The Hand of God*, in plaster, was
probably exhibited in Munich
in 1896. There are several marble
copies of this work; this one
was sculpted in 1916 for the future
Rodin Museum.

39

41

41 **Rodin and Henriette Coltat in front of *The Gates of Hell*,** photograph by Pierre Choumoff, 22.8 x 17.3 cm. Inv. Ph. 823.

42 ***The Gates of Hell*,** 1880-1917 (cast between 1919 and 1929), bronze, 635 x 400 x 85 cm. Inv. S. 1304. Photo B. Jarret.

In 1880 the State commissioned a monumental bronze from Rodin for the future Decorative Arts Museum, although its location had not yet been determined. Rodin himself seems to have chosen this theme from Dante's *Divine Comedy*. The door would include Rodin's interpretation of the dramatic scenes of Hell, giving him the chance to express passion, violence and despair. Rodin's initial inspiration came from the Baptistery doors in Florence, but he eliminated the geometric division of the panels, keeping only the lintel and two doors covered with a mass of interconnected figures. The relief of these figures produces spectacular effects of light and shadow. Rodin worked furiously on *The Gates* in the early 1880s, and by 1884 the work had advanced far enough so that he requested an estimate for the casting. But around 1888-89, other commissions started to sidetrack the artist from this work and it became clear that the group would never be completed. The model exhibited in 1900 had almost no figures modeled in the round (this work is now in the Meudon Museum). The final work is in the Orsay Museum as the bronzes were cast only after Rodin's death (the first copy was in 1926).

47

détails of **The Gates of Hell**:
43 **Ugolin,** 44 **The Falling Man,**
45 **The Thinker,** 46 **Fugit Amor.**
Photo B. Jarret.

47 **Adam,**
1881, bronze, 194 x 74 x 74 cm.
Inv. S. 962. Photo A. Rzepka.

The Gates of Hell provided Rodin
with a chance to create a range of
subjects that he developed
separately and which became
famous as individual works in
themselves. This is true, of course,
for *The Thinker* and *The Kiss*,
but also for *Ugolin, Fugit Amor,
The Falling Man, The Danaide, The
Martyr, Caryatid and the Stone,
The Prodigal Son* and the
many variations on the figures of
the damned.

44

45

46

48 **The Cathedral,**
1908, stone, 64 x 29.5 x 31.8 cm.
Inv. S. 1001. Photo E. and P. Hesmerg.

49 **The Secret,**
1909, marble, 89 x 49.7 x 40.7 cm.
Inv. S. 1000. Photo B. Jarret.

"There are hands in Rodin's work, small, independent hands that are alive, even though unconnected to any body. Hands that stand straight up, or are irritated and bad ... hands that walk and sleep and hands that wake up; criminal hands ... and hands that are tired..." (Rilke). There are also hands assembled with other hands: *The Secret* and *The Cathedral* are both formed

of two right hands to avoid an ungraceful opposition of the same fingers. While the hands in the first work enclose an empty space – Rodin created it in reference to the Gothic cathedrals he loved so much – those in the second surround a block of marble sculpted like a box or a chalice. The work had a symbolic meaning. "A hand that touches," continued Rilke, "no longer totally belongs [to the body] from which it came. It and the object it touches or grasps together form something new, something else that has no name and that belongs to no one."

48

Plasters of Meudon

On December 19, 1898, after moving several times, Rodin purchased the Villa des Brillants in Meudon. He was very fond of this modest home and constantly expanded his property by buying up adjoining lots; the existing buildings were transformed into studios for his *praticiens* and casters. In 1901, he had the Pavillon de l'Alma reconstructed alongside the verandah. This pavilion, erected for the 1900 Universal Exposition, housed the large retrospective show of Rodin's works that ushered in his immense popularity. The building, which we can only see in photographs as it was destroyed, became something of a studio/museum where Rodin could show visitors the many sculptures he stored within it. In a way, it was a forerunner to the Rodin Museum in Paris, a project the artist had started to develop; it began to take shape through his bequest to the State in 1916. Other changes to Rodin's property included the facade

of the Château of Issy-les-Moulineaux, which had burned down in 1871; Rodin had it reconstructed in 1907-08. The tomb of the sculptor and his companion Rose Beuret lies in front of these seventeenth-century vestiges. A statue of *The Thinker* overlooks the artist's resting place.

The appearance of the property changed after Rodin's death. The Pavillon de l'Alma was replaced by the current building, which was constructed between 1929 and 1931 by the architect Henry Favier. It was funded by a gift from an American, Jules Mastbaum, founder of the Rodin Museum in Philadelphia. The other buildings also disappeared, which made the property more open, but also deprived it of its documentary character. The museum opened in 1947 and was recently restored.

The thousands of plaster and terra-cotta models created by Rodin throughout his career are in

50 **Overall view of the studio in Meudon.** Photo A. Rzepka.

51 **Rodin in his studio, in the middle of the plaster casts,** anonymous photograph, 1902, 25.3 x 25 cm. Inv. Ph. 203.

52

53

Meudon, along with the casts used to make these plaster works. A certain number of these plaster casts are on public display, thereby providing insight into the genesis of his most famous works. The studies for *The Gates of Hell* are obviously among the most interesting works to see at the museum. It is possible to see some of the isolated figures before they were added to the composition. Several display cases show examples of the preliminary work undertaken for a version of *The Gates*. It shows the work without the relief figures, as it was exhibited at the 1900 Universal Exposition.

Aside from the original plaster casts, the studies for such major works as *The Burghers of Calais* are the most interesting. For the figure of *Balzac*, for example, there are several busts created from various documents that the sculptor had collected, along with several full-length versions,

with the figure on a pedestal, nude or clothed, and even an amazing study of the dressing gown, all works that preceded the completion of the final statue. These plaster models shed light on the work of the sculptor, who did not limit himself to modeling techniques only. He assembled limbs and bodies that had been designed separately, without worrying about the differences in the surfaces. Pieces of fabric dipped in plaster were used to drape the figures to find the final composition. His process was identical for the various versions of the *Monument to Victor Hugo*. His hesitations concerning the grouping of subjects are all visible and the various compositions reflect the artist's unsatisfactory research.

These plaster models provide insight into Rodin's method of working, as he left no written explanations. Through them we can learn

54

about his innovative methods, although this aspect is less visible in the final works. The unique aspect of the Rodin Museum in Meudon is that it provides a complementary view of the artist with respect to the Paris museum, which primarily exhibits sculptures executed in more noble materials, such as bronze or marble.

Nevertheless, we still do not have a definitive list of all of Rodin's work. The lengthy task of compiling an inventory of the storerooms has yielded wonderful surprises. An entire aspect of Rodin's creation that has so far remained concealed is coming to light, particularly the role of assemblage, which he used almost systematically in the last years of his career. When Rodin was creating *The Gates of Hell* he took some of the figures that he had designed for it and depicted them in different positions – one such example is *The Martyr*. We also know that he made use of multiples, such *The Three Shades*. He took increasing liberties with his assemblages by adding incongruous elements – branches (one of these is found in the assemblages of two figures, *Eve* and *The Crouching Woman*) or elements from antique ceramics in his collection – to the castings of the models. He thus created the foundations of twentieth-century sculpture. It is easier to understand Rodin's influence on the young sculptors of his day.

This extremely contemporary aspect is being shown to the public. Certain pieces were recently exhibited at temporary exhibits and a larger number of these are on display at the Meudon Museum. We are fortunate for Rodin's bequest to the State; the fate of these plasters would otherwise have been precarious, because at the time, only finished works were appreciated. Today, the plaster pieces reflect the love and understanding of sculpture that, above all, consists of forms arranged in space.

Nicole Barbier

55

The Drawings

The fame of Rodin's drawings is paradoxical. The image that comes to mind is a nude female in a somewhat lascivious pose, drawn with a light stroke and highlighted with watercolors in shades of sienna. Unfortunately, many forgeries also fulfill this description; to correct this view and to educate the public, the Rodin Museum is publishing his complete works, which includes some 7,200 drawings. As a whole, these works are astonishing in their variety and subtlety. Although Rodin drew before sculpting his models, it was not only because he had a sculpture in mind.

The works from his early years reflect a taste for antiquity and ornamentation: red-chalk landscapes occupied him during a visit to Belgium. A trip to Italy and the discovery of Michelangelo were decisive events for Rodin and deepened his interest in Dante's *Inferno*. That was the romantic, visionary age of the draftsman, in which life's tragic side was expressed through the murky tangle of pencils, pen, brown wash and gouache. His depictions of *The Divine Comedy* were literal, and his drawings were much closer to the book than his sculptures; although the first did not necessarily lead to the second, they could not have come alive without them. From Dante's tormented souls to Baudelaire's *Femmes damnées*, the spiritual connection is clear. Each of these two poets battled with the other in Rodin's imagination when, in 1887, Paul Gallimard commissioned the artist to illustrate *Les Fleurs du mal*. The drawings that Rodin sketched in the margins of this single copy were only seen by a very small circle of art-lovers. The facsimile editions of 1918, 1940, 1968 and 1983 made them available to a wider public. The 1897 Goupil Album (named after the publisher of prints) was distributed to no more than the 125 subscribers. In it, Octave Mirbeau underlined the confidential nature of the work in a preface to the 142 drawings inspired by Dante. Maurice Fenaille, a great admirer of Rodin, was at the origin of this project. During the period he was planning *The Gates of Hell*, Rodin traveled extensively

55 *Dawn, reclining nude woman with hands behind her head,* ca. 1900, lead pencil, watercolor and gouache on beige paper, 32.4 x 24.7 cm. Inv. D. 5006. Photo B. Jarret.

56 *Pysche Transported to Heaven,* 1898-1907, lead pencil, stump and watercolor on cream paper, 32.5 x 25.2 cm. Inv. D. 4606. Photo B. Jarret.

56

57

throughout France, choosing to sketch simpler churches than great cathedrals; he reproduced hundreds of moldings in his notebooks. In 1914, he published some of his architectural drawings in a volume entitled *Cathédrales de France*, prefaced by Charles Morice.

Rodin, a man of shadow and light, gradually lightened his palette and started using women as models, a subject he never grew tired of. The size of the paper became larger, the pencil line and brushwork calmer. He avoided unbridled exaltation and limited himself to an observation of life. Critics believe that they have detected in these drawings an inspiration from the Grecian urn painters or Japanese woodblock artists. In February 1899, Vollard signed a contract with Rodin for the illustration of Mirbeau's *Jardin des Supplices*. The lithographer Auguste Clot transferred Rodin's watercolors onto the stone. The media was frightened by the bold poses and the strokes executed in a single line. Rodin was both hailed as a genius and accused of creating nothing more than hasty sketches. The titles of the drawings were often inspired from mythology, particularly Ovid's *Metamorphoses*. Rodin became the tireless interpreter of the body and its movements, depicted on thousands of bits of paper. He was attracted to modern dance that had cast off the fetters of the Western world while adhering to Far Eastern traditions. Rodin's discovery of the Cambodian ballet troupe at the 1908 Colonial Exposition resulted in a dazzling series of drawings.

Using pencils and stump, which he often applied with his fingers, Rodin devoted painstaking, passionate attention to sketching delicate and subtle watercolors of female models. His drawings, which were already included in private collections, were exhibited in Paris and abroad. From Europe to America, the major world capitals were discovering and appreciating a entirely new approach to the art of

58

59

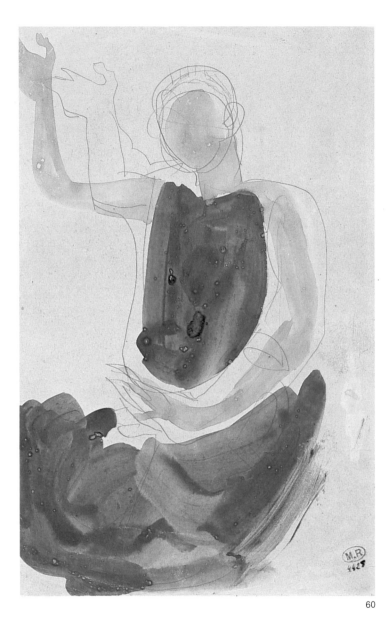

60

drawing. And Rodin kept to himself works he felt he could not show to his contemporaries; these drawings the découpages and the erotic sketches are now highly valued. The experiments with three-dimensional paper works – a natural outlet for a sculptor – were repeated many years later by a painter named Matisse. As for his Hell, which no longer corresponded to Dante's Inferno, it became a more compulsive subject for Rodin as he grew older. This was an inclination he shared with Victor Hugo, another poet whose path lay parallel to Rodin's own.

The publication of the five volumes of the inventory of the drawings, which was completed in 1992, reflects the Rodin Museum's concern to show works to the general public that must be stored in boxes away from daylight, due to the fragility of the drawings. The final volume includes the recent acquisitions – which will add rare or missing items to the collections – a transcription of 55 annotated notebooks, a bibliography, a list of drawings exhibited during Rodin's lifetime, and an index. One room in the Hôtel Biron is reserved for a rotating exhibition

61

of these drawings; they are changed every three months. Specific exhibitions are organized around certain themes.

With Rodin's drawings, there remains the ongoing problem of dating his works. He himself was quite careless in this respect and the only solution had been to resort to highly oblique methods or to proceed by necessarily hazardous hunches. The various periods of his creative activity are fairly easy to determine; details concerning the chronology of his work, however, are harder to determine. **Claudie Judrin**

Rodin photographed

62 ***Monument to Victor Hugo*** **in the Palais-Royal gardens,** photograph by Adolphe Braun, 21.5 x 27.5 cm. Inv. Ph. 1194.

63 ***Eternal Spring,*** photograph by Jacques-Ernest Bulloz, 27 x 36 cm. Inv. Ph. 1582.

63

The photography collection in the Rodin Museum contains some 8,000 images, mostly of Rodin and his work. Some three-fourths of the collection are photographs of sculptures, commissioned by Rodin from various photographers: the most famous names along with unknown ones, including Steichen, Bulloz, Druet, Coburn, Haweis, Coles, as well as Pannelier, Bodmer and Freuler. Despite the sculptor's demands with regard to lighting, shooting angles and backgrounds, each of these photographers brought a new vision to the works.

In additions to these photographs, which are doubly interesting as documents and aesthetic objects, there are the many portraits of Rodin posing alone (by Nadar, Steichen, Kazebier and Coburn); in the company of close friends, professional associates and society acquaintances; and photographs of his student's sculptures, submitted for his criticism. At Rodin's death, the museum's first curator, Léonce Bénédite, built up the general archives by adding photographs of sculptures, paintings and architecture from various periods.

It is important to continue the sculptor's process by adding to the collection and exhibiting work from it. In 1985, five photographers (Tom Drahos, Kiuston Hallé, Bruno Jarret, Bernadette Tintaud and Holger Trülsch) were invited to give their interpretations of Rodin's work. Thematic or monographic exhibitions have revealed the extent of the collection. These include photographs commissioned by Rodin to promote his work; photographs of dancers who met the artist (including Isadora Duncan, Loïe Fuller and Ruth Saint Denis); autochromes by Etienne Clémentel; the sculptor's models; and even contemporary photographs by Myriam and Gilles Arnould, Isabel Formosa and Bruno Jarret of the many sculptures in the museum's storerooms. **Hélène Pinet**

64

65

66

64 **Rodin,** *The Thinker* **and** *Monument to Victor Hugo,* photograph by Edward Steichen, 1902, 26 x 32 cm. Inv. Ph. 217.

65 *The Thinker,* photograph by Jean-François Limet, 37 x 27.3 cm. Inv. Ph. 980.

66 *Pierre de Wissant,* photograph by Edward Steichen, 20.5 x 13.2 cm. Inv. Ph. 425.

67 *Balzac,* photograph by Edward Steichen, 15.6 x 19 cm. Inv. Ph. 255.

Biography

1840. Francois-Auguste René Rodin was born on the November 12 in Paris, at 3, rue de l'Arbalète.

1847. Rodin studied religious instruction at the school of the Frères de La Doctrine chrétienne, rue du Val-de-Grâce. He began to draw at the age of nine.

1854. He enrolled in the Ecole Impériale de Dessin et de Mathématiques (La Petite Ecole), now the Advanced School for Decorative Arts. He took courses from Lecoq de Boisbaudran, who taught drawing from memory and made copies of works by eighteenth-century French artists, including Boucher, Van Loo, Bouchardon and Clodion, as well as drawing antiquities in the Louvre and prints from the royal library. He also attended classes in life drawing at the Ecole de la Manufacture des Gobelins, and classes in literature and history at the Collège de France. He began reading works by Michelet, Victor Hugo, Musset, Homer, Dante and Virgile.

1857. On the advice of the sculptor Maindron, who had noticed his drawings, Rodin took the admission exam for the sculpture section at the Ecole des Beaux-Arts, but was rejected three times because of his style, considered to be overly influenced by the eighteenth century.

1858. In order to help support his family, he worked as a molder and ornamenter for several decorators. Remembering the time he spent working for the plasterer Simon, Rodin later noted that Simon had taught him the "science of modeling." In 1860, he completed a bust of his father, an austere neo-classical portrait, his first known work.

1862. Rodin was deeply affected by the death of his sister Marie. He joined the Order of the Fathers of the Holy Sacrament as a novice.

1863. Rodin sculpted a bust of Father Eymard, who encouraged him to pursue a career as a sculptor. Rodin left the religious order in late May. He rented a stable near the Gobelins tapestry manufacture, which he arranged as a studio, and began to work on the *Man with the Broken Nose*. The plaster model submitted to the Salon jury the following year was refused. He joined the Central Union of Decorative Arts, whose membership included Delacroix, Ingres, Lecoq de Boisbaudran, Dumas Père, and Théophile Gautier. There he made the acquaintance of Carpeaux, who subsequently treated him rather coldly in his studio.

1864. Rodin studied with Barye at the Museum of Natural History and took anatomy courses at the medical school. He met Rose Beuret, who modeled for him and who shared the rest of his life, becoming his wife shortly before his death. He worked on the decoration of the Théâtre des Gobelins, the Panorama des Champs-Elysées and the Théâtre de la Gaieté. He met Carrier-Belleuse and worked part-time as a modeler under the latter's supervision at the Sèvres Porcelain factory.

1865. He rented a studio on Rue Lebrun. He worked on the decoration of La Païva's town house on the Avenue des Champs-Elysées.

1866. Birth of Rodin's son, Auguste-Eugène Beuret, on January 18.

1870. During the Franco-Prussian war, was drafted into the 150th regiment of the national guard, but was soon discharged because of his myopia.

1871. After the armistice, Rodin joined Carrier-Belleuse in Brussels and under his supervision worked on the decoration of the Belgian Royal Exchange.

1872. Rose joined him in Brussels. Rodin executed models for the Compagnie des Bronzes.

1875. Rodin exhibited at the Salon des Artistes in Paris and competed in a contest for the *Monument to Lord Byron* in London. He traveled to Italy in the winter.

1876. Rodin visited Florence and Rome, and copied works by Donatello and Michelangelo. After returning to Brussels, he started working on *The Age of Bronze*, using live models. He sculptured a group entitled *Ugolino and his Children*, which was immediately destroyed. At the Philadelphia Centennial Exhibition, he displayed his models produced for the Compagnie des Bronzes.

1877. Rodin displayed the plaster model of *the Age of Bronze* under the title of *The Vanquished*, at the Cercle Artistique in Brussels, and subsequently at the Salon in Paris. Despite his protests, he was accused of having molded this sculpture directly from a live model. However, the work created a sensation among the students at the Ecole des Beaux-Arts. Rodin and Rose returned to Paris in the autumn, after visiting several French cathedrals. He made preliminary drawings for *St. John the Baptist Preaching*, while continuing to work for jewelers, cabinetmakers and the sculptor Laouste (decorator of the palace of the Trocadéro).

1878. The sculptors Dupuis, Chapu, Carrier-Belleuse, Chaplain and Falguière, among others, sent a letter to the minister to defend Rodin in the "affair" of *The Age of Bronze*.

1879. At the invitation of Carrier-Belleuse, who had become the director of the Sèvres porcelain factory, Rodin was appointed as a member of the temporary special staff. He worked there at irregular intervals until late 1882.

1880. At the Salon, Rodin exhibited the plaster model of *St. John the Baptist Preaching* and the bronze statue of *The Age of Bronze*, which received an honorable mention and was purchased by the State. Edmond Turquet, the undersecretary of state for the Beaux-Arts, commissioned Rodin to produce a monumental door for a Decorative Arts Museum to be built in Paris. Rodin started working on *The Gates of Hell*. The door was never finished, although it occupied Rodin over a 30-year period and included some of his most famous works. He obtained an atelier at the Marble Depot.

1881. *St. John the Baptist Preaching* was purchased by the State after being exhibited at the Salon. Rodin made the first of several trips to London at the invitation of Alphonse Legros. The latter initiated him into the art of drypoint engraving and introduced him to W. E. Henley, the director of the *Magazine of Art* which contributed to Rodin's fame in England.

1882. Rodin began a major series of busts of his artist and writer friends (including Carrier-Belleuse, Laurens, Dalou, Haquette, Becque and Hugo).

1883. Rodin met Camille Claudel, who became his student, mistress, collaborator and model for nearly 15 years.

1884. Rodin rented a large atelier at 117, rue de Vaugirard. He divided his time between his project for *The Burghers of Calais* and *The Gates of Hell*.

1885. The city of Calais commissioned Rodin to sculpt *The Burghers of Calais*. First portrait of Camille Claudel, *Dawn*.

1886. Rodin moved again, this time to 71, rue de Bourgogne. He won the competition for the *Monument to Bastien-Lepage* at Damvilliers (unveiled in 1889). He prepared a series of drawings to illustrate Baudelaire's *Fleurs du mal* (1887-88) and displayed a large number of works at the first international exhibition of the Georges Petit gallery. He created a second portrait of Camille Claudel, *The Thought*, and *The Kiss*.

1887. On 31 December, Rodin was granted the rank of Chevalier of the Legion of Honor. He became an officier in 1892, then a commander in 1903.

1888. The State commissioned Rodin to produce a marble replica of *The Kiss*, and purchased the *Bust of Madame Morla Vicuña*. Rodin rented the Folie Neubourg, a house on the boulevard d'Italie, where he spent most of his time with Camille Claudel.

1889. On April 9, Rodin received a commission to design a *Monument to Claude Lorrain* for the city of Nancy. He was elected to the jury of the Salon and the jury for the Universal Exposition. The exhibitions of his works at the Universal Exhibition and at the Georges Petit gallery (36 sculptures, including all the figures of *The Burghers of Calais*, shown for the first time), which occured simultaneously with Monet's paintings, greatly contributed to Rodin's reputation. The most prominent critics became his defenders: Camille Mauclair, Gustave Geffroy, Octave Mirbeau and Roger Marx. On September 16, he was commissioned by the State to sculpt a *Monument to Victor Hugo* for the Pantheon. He worked on this during the winter, but ignored the instructions of the administration, which had ordered a standing figure. He chose to represent Hugo seated, surrounded by the Muses. The following year, this sculpture was deemed unsuitable for the planned site; in early 1891, however, there were tentative plans to install it in the Luxembourg Gardens.

1890. Rodin rented Scribe's former residence in Bellevue-Sèvres. Together with Dalou, Meissonier, Carrière and Puvis de Chavannes, he founded the National Society of Fine Arts. He was elected vice-president of the sculpture section. During the winter, he began work on the second *Monument to Victor Hugo* for the Pantheon.

1891. The Société des Gens de Lettres commissioned him to sculpt *Balzac*, a work to be delivered within 18 months.

1892. The *Monument to Claude Lorrain*, dedicated on June 6 in Nancy, was severely

69 **Rodin at the Fourth Exhibition of the New Gallery,** photograph by the Stereoscopic Company, London, 24 x 28.6 cm. Inv. Ph. 1923.

70 **Rodin surrounded by Léonce Bénédite, Mlle Coltat and unidentifed figure,** photograph by Pierre Choumoff, 22 x 16.7 cm. Inv. Ph. 895.

criticized. Rodin had to modify the pedestal. A subscription launched by Leconte de Lisle was opened for a monument to Baudelaire to be made by Rodin. The first book devoted to Rodin was published, written by Gustave Geffroy.

1894. The Société des Gens de Lettres issued Rodin a formal summons to deliver the *Balzac*. He traveled to southern France and visited Monet in Giverny, with Clémenceau, Mirbeau, Geffroy and Cézanne.

1895. Rodin purchased the Villa des Brillants in Meudon, which was to be his principal residence until his death. He was in poor health and depressed, and obliged to cope with the criticism of a large part of the press that had taken up the controversy over the statue of *Balzac*. *The Burghers of Calais* was dedicated, although it was not installed according to Rodin's instructions.

1896. The Rath Museum in Geneva received Rodin's gift of three sculptures, one of which was judged indecent and was relegated to the basement storage room.

1897. The Goupil publishing house issued the first major study of Rodin's drawings, with a preface by Mirbeau.

1898. Rodin broke off with Camille Claudel. The Société des Gens de Lettres refused the statue of Balzac (exhibited at the Salon), considering it to be unfinished. Rodin's detractors waged a press campaign against him.

1899. Rodin was commissioned to design a monument to Puvis de Chavannes. In the spring, he traveled to Belgium and Holland with Judith Cladel, who had organized a large traveling exhibition through these countries.

1900. During the Universal Exposition, Rodin exhibited 150 works in a pavilion on the Place de l'Alma, made possible through the financial assistance of his admirers. This hugely successful show brought him international renown. He received commissions for sculptures from foreign museums as well as from private collectors, notably American and English. The statue of *Sarmiento* (president of Argentina) unveiled in Buenos Aires met with hostility from the public and the press.

1901. After a decade of intense activity devoted to major projects that earned him many detractors, he concentrated on doing busts and small sculptures, including figures of dancers. He devoted more of his time to drawing, and to supervising his many assistants producing the marble copies of his sculptures. With two of them, Jules Desbois and Antoine Bourdelle, he founded the Académie Rodin on Boulevard du Montparnasse. He exhibited at the Venice Biennale and the third Secession show in Berlin.

1902. Rodin was visited in Meudon by Edward Steichen, who proceeded to photograph his works. Rodin went to London for a banquet held in his honor, and was carried in triumph by the students of the Slade School of Art. He traveled to Prague for the inauguration of an exhibition of his works organized by the Manes Society. He met Rainer Maria Rilke in September and began

69

70

to correspond with him. Alexis Rudier became Rodin's principal caster.

1903. Publication of two important books: *Auguste Rodin*, by Rainer Maria Rilke and *Auguste Rodin: Pris sur la vie*, by Judith Cladel. After the death of Whistler (for whom he had begun a statue), Rodin was elected president of

the International Society of Painters, Sculptors and Engravers.

1904. Rodin met Claire Coudert, duchesse de Choiseul, the "muse" who would dominate his life over the ensuing eight years and would manage to estrange him from most of his loyal friends.

1905. Rilke became Rodin's secretary. He had exhibitions at the Copley Society in Boston and at the Venice Biennale. *The Thinker* was erected in front of the Pantheon (in 1922, it was moved to the musée Rodin). With Rilke and the painter Ignacio Zuloaga, Rodin traveled to Spain, visiting Toledo, Madrid, Cordoba, Seville and Pamplona.

1906. Rodin dismissed Rilke and replaced him with the Englishman Anthony Ludovici. Rodin was enthusiastic about the Paris performances of the royal Cambodian Ballet and showed great interest in dance by frequenting Isadora Duncan's school.

1907. Rodin was awarded the degree of Doctor honoris causa from Oxford University. The first major exhibition of his drawings was held at the Bernheim Jeune gallery in Paris. His works were exhibited in Barcelona, Budapest, London, New York, Venice and Berlin.

1908. King Edward VII of England visited Rodin in Meudon. Rodin installed himself on the ground floor of the Hôtel Biron on Rue de Varenne.

1909. A modified version of the first *Monument to Victor Hugo* was erected in the Palais Royal gardens.

1910. A special issue of *Camera Work* magazine was devoted to Rodin.

1911. The Hôtel Biron was purchased by the State. Judith Cladel and Gustave Coquiot proposed the creation of a Rodin Museum in this building. Many artists, writers and politicians backed the plan.

1912. Rodin went to Rome to inspect the planned site of his *Walking Man*, which a group of admirers hoped to erect in the courtyard of the Farnese palace, the home of the French embassy. The ambassador opposed the plan, and the statue was shipped to Lyon. Rodin presented 18 plaster models to the Metropolitan Museum of Art. His defense of the ballet *The Afternoon of a Faun*, danced by Nijinsky, provoked a new scandal. He severed his relationship with the duchesse de Choiseul. The decline of his mental faculties triggered self-serving intrigues among his intimates bent on gaining control over his works.

1913. Seven of Rodin's drawings were exhibited at the Armory show in New York. Publication of a book by H. Dujardin-Beaumetz, *Entretiens avec Rodin*. The Burghers of Calais was installed in the Victoria Gardens in London.

1914. Publication of *Cathédrales de France*. Rodin's health deteriorated and he went to southern France to rest. He traveled to London for exhibitions at Grosvenor House, the duke of Westminster's residence, and at the Victoria and Albert Museum.

1915. Trip to Rome, where Rodin sculpted a portrait of Pope Benedict XV.

1916. Rodin became gravely ill. He gave to the French government all his works for the Rodin Museum to be installed in the Hôtel Biron. His friends, particularly Judith Cladel and Etienne Clémentel, defended his interests against the intrigues that were being plotted around him. On September 14, by 381 votes to 52, the Chamber of Deputies passed a law instituting "definitive acceptance of the deed of gift to the State by Auguste Rodin." On September 22, both houses of the French parliament ratified the acceptance of the donation of the Hôtel Biron. The legal status and financial autonomy of the Rodin Museum were determined by the law of June 28, 1918.

1917. On January 29, in Meudon, Rodin married Rose Beuret, who died on February 14. On October 30, Léon Bonnat and François Flameng offered him membership in the French Institute. Rodin passed away on November 17 and his funeral was held in Meudon on November 24. He was buried beside Rose Beuret in front of the reconstructed facade of the château of Issy-les-Moulineaux, with the statue of *The Thinker* over his grave.

1919. The Rodin Museum opened to the public.

Bibliography

This is a selection of the many books written about Rodin.
A complete bibliography was drawn up by Joseph Adolf Schmollgen. Eisenwerth
in *Rodin Studien,* published in 1983.

● Rainer Maria Rilke, *Lettres à Rodin*, préface de Georges Grappe, Emile-Paul Frères, Paris, 1931.

● Georges Grappe, *Catalogue du musée Rodin, hôtel Biron. Essai de classement chronologique des œuvres d'Auguste Rodin*, Paris, 1944, 5ᵉ édition.

● Albert E. Elsen, *Rodin's Gates of Hell*, University of Minnesota Press, Minneapolis,1960.

● Denys Sutton, *Triumphant Satyr: The World of Auguste Rodin*, Country, Londres, 1966.

● Albert E. Elsen, *The Drawings of Rodin*, Praeger Publishers, New York, 1971.

● Albert E. Elsen, *Rodin*, Secker & Warburg, Londres, 1974.

● Victoria Thorson, *Rodin's Graphics. Catalogue Raisonné of Drypoints and Book Illustrations*, Fine Arts Museum, San Francisco, 1975.

● John L. Tancock, *The Sculpture of Auguste Rodin*, Philadephia Museum of Art, 1976.

● Ruth Butler, *Rodin in perspective*, by Prentice-Hall Inc., Englewood Cliffs, New Jersey, 1980.

● Albert E. Elsen, *Dans l'atelier de Rodin*, Phaïdon/Musée Rodin, Oxford, 1980.

● Paul Gsell, *l'Art. Entretiens réunis par Paul Gsell*, Grasset, Paris, 1981 (1ᵉ édition, 1911).

● Claudie Judrin, *Auguste Rodin, Dessins et Aquarelles*, Editions Hervas, Paris, 1982.

● Josef Adolf Schmollgen. Eisenwerth, *Rodin Studien*, Prestel Verlag, München, 1983.

● Albert E. Elsen, *Rodin's Thinker and the Dilemnas of Modern Public Sculpture*, Yale University Press, New Haven & Londres, 1985.

● Monique Laurent, *le Musée Rodin*, Hazan, Paris, 1986.

● Nicole Barbier, *Marbres de Rodin. Collection du musée*, Editions du Musée Rodin, Paris, 1987.

● Philippe Sollers, Alain Kirili, *Rodin. Dessins érotiques*, Gallimard, Paris, 1987.

● Frédéric V. Grunfeld, *Rodin*, Arthème Fayard, Paris, 1988.

● Hélène Pinet, *Auguste Rodin, les Mains du Génie*, Gallimard, Paris, 1988.

● Cécile Goldscheider, *Rodin. Catalogue raisonné*, tome I, Institut Wildenstein, Paris, 1989.

● Claudie Judrin, *Inventaire des dessins du musée Rodin*, 5 tomes, musée Rodin, Paris, 1984-1992.

● Ruth Butler, *The Shape of Genius*, Yale University Press, 1993.

● Claudie Judrin, *Quatre-vingt dessins de Rodin*, musée Rodin/R.M.N., Paris, 1995.

● Antoinette Lenormand-Romain, *le Baiser*, Musée Rodin/RMN, Paris, 1995.

Catalogues of Exhibitions at the Rodin Museum

● *Rodin et les écrivains de son temps*, Paris, 1975.

● *Auguste Rodin. Les Monuments des Bourgeois de Calais 1884-1895 dans les collections du musée Rodin et du musée des Beaux-Arts de Calais*, Paris-Calais, 1977.

● *Rodin et l'Extrême-Orient*, Paris, 1979.

● *Les Centaures, Cabinet des dessins I*, Paris, 1981.

● *Ugolin, Cabinet des dessins II*, Paris, 1982.

● *Dante et Virgile aux Enfers, Cabinet des dessins III*, Paris 1983.

● *Monet, Rodin*, Paris, 1989.

● *Rodin sculpteur*, Paris, 1993.

● *Rodin, Whistler et la Muse*, Paris, 1994.

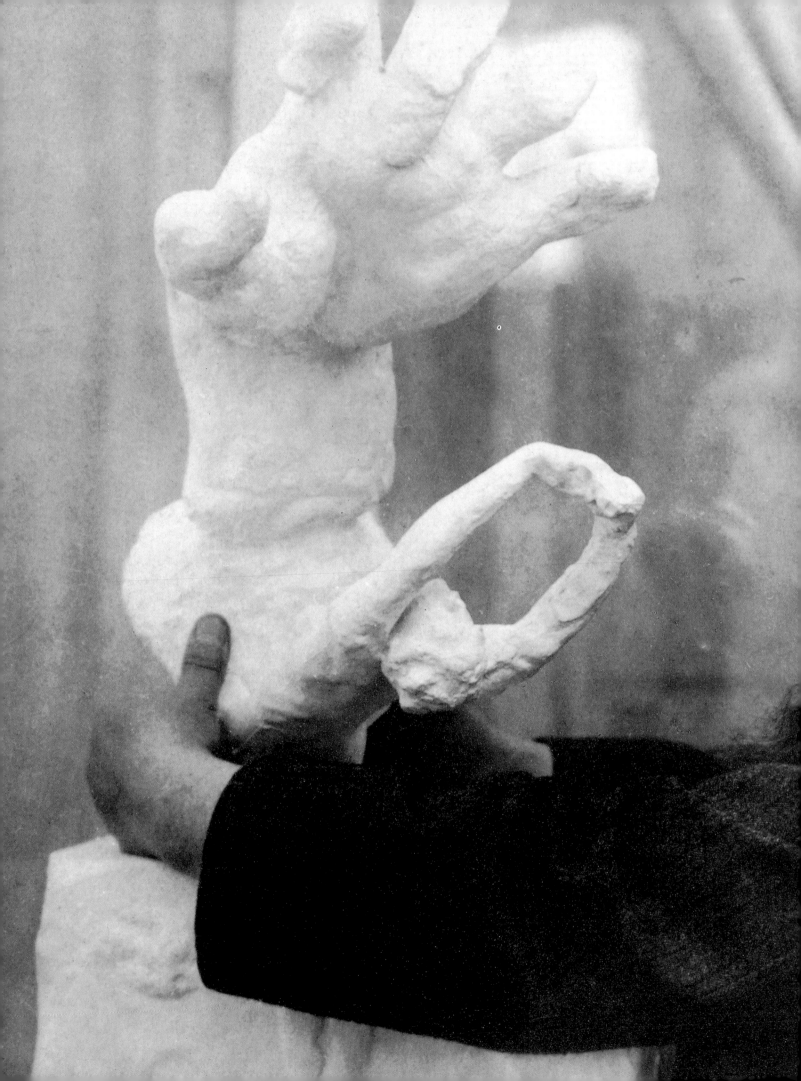